JONAS VINGEGAARD
BIOGRAPHY

How He Became a Cycling Champion

Shara A. Wolff

Disclaimer

This book is planned to give supportive data on web security for kids. It doesn't supplant direction from guardians, gatekeepers, or instructors. While each work has been made to guarantee precision, the quickly changing nature of innovation implies that a few subtleties might become obsolete. Continuously counsel a believed grown-up for guidance on remaining safe on the web, and recall that internet based security is a common obligation. The writer and distributor are not responsible for any activities taken in view of the substance of this book.

Copyright

No piece of this book might be imitated, circulated, or sent in any structure or using any and all means, including copying, recording, or other electronic or mechanical techniques, without the earlier composed consent of the distributer, with the exception of brief citations encapsulated in basic audits and certain other noncommercial purposes allowed by intellectual property regulation.

Copyright © 2024 by Shara A. Wolff Protected by copyright law

Table of contents

INTRODUCTION
CHAPTER 1 EARLY DAYS OF JONAS
CHAPTER 2 THE START OF A CYCLING JOURNEY
CHAPTER 3 TRAINING HARD
CHAPTER 4 BIG RACES AND ACHIEVEMENTS
CHAPTER 5 LIFE AS A CHAMPION
CHAPTER 6 JONAS TIPS FOR YOUNG CYCLISTS
CONCLUSION

INTRODUCTION

Envision riding a bicycle so quick that it seems like you're flying! That is precisely the exact thing Jonas Vingegaard does each time he races. Jonas is a very cool cyclist from Denmark who has come out on top in enormous races and become a genuine boss. Be that as it may, how could he get so astonishing at trekking? We should take a tomfoolery ride through his life to find out!

Jonas was very much like whatever other youngster who cherished playing and investigating. In any case, rather than longing for being a superhuman or a renowned performer, Jonas had a unique dream: he needed to be a top cyclist. He began with a straightforward bike and a major grin, and with loads of training and difficult work, he transformed that fantasy into the real world.

you'll advance about Jonas' thrilling excursion from a young man who cherished cycling to turning into a popular hero who races in the greatest contests. You'll figure out how he rehearsed, what challenges he confronted, and the stuff to turn into a champ. Thus, lock in your safety belt, or would it be advisable for me I say, attach your protective cap, and prepare to pedal through the astonishing story of Jonas Vingegaard!

Jonas Vingegaard didn't just transform into a cycling champion for now. It took a lot of troublesome work, confirmation, and energy. All things considered, what makes Jonas such an exceptional cyclist?

Most importantly, Jonas loves cycling more than anything. Right when he was more energetic, he went through hours riding his bike around his region, feeling the breeze in his hair and the energy of the ride. This warmth for cycling gave him the energy to practice reliably and never give up, regardless, when it was outrageous.

Second, Jonas is remarkably engaged. He didn't just ride his bike for amusement; he arranged really hard to transform into the best. He followed unprecedented exercises to make his legs strong and dominated new capacities to be impressively faster. His coaches helped him with learning the unpretentious systems and further foster his hustling methodology.

Third, Jonas is truly locked in. In each race, he remains completely composed and gives close thought to the track. He knows how to take on a consistent speed, when to go fast, and when to save his energy. This middle helps him with chasing after insightful decisions during races and gives him the edge over his adversaries.

At long last, Jonas will not at any point give up. There were times when he faced extraordinary troubles, for example, getting broken down or overseeing wounds. Regardless, he for the most part stayed positive and kept on pushing forward. His affirmation and trust in himself helped him with overcoming obstacles and achieving his dreams.

Along these lines, whether he's hustling in a significant contention or basically playing with his sidekicks, Jonas' reverence for cycling, troublesome work, focus, and never-give-up demeanor make him a certifiable cycling champion.

CHAPTER 1 EARLY DAYS OF JONAS

Jonas Vingegaard was brought into the world in an agreeable town in Denmark, where he grew up enveloped by a lovely open nation and very much arranged people. From the get-go, Jonas was a valiant and curious youth. He esteemed examining the outside and contributing energy with his friends and family.

Jonas' most significant bike was a little, red one that he got when he was a smidgen of youngsters. He didn't know it by then, but that red bike would be the start of something surprising. Reliably after school, Jonas would ride his bike around the area, feeling free and bright. His people and colleagues saw the sum he savored the experience of cycling and encouraged him to keep on riding.

As Jonas aged significantly, his energy for cycling just got more grounded. He joined a local cycling club where he met various youngsters who esteemed traveling a lot like him. Together, they would go on fun rides and work on hustling skills. Jonas loved the impression of riding fast and endeavoring to surpass his mates in pleasant challenges.

In spite of the way that he was energetic, Jonas yearned for transforming into an uncommon cyclist. He watched cycling races on TV and valued the supervisors he saw. He imagined himself riding in those colossal races one day and winning shining honors.

Jonas' underlying days were stacked up with fun bike rides and colossal dreams. His reverence for cycling and the assistance from his friends and family helped him with getting everything moving while heading to transforming into a cycling champion.

Encountering youth in Denmark looked like living in a storybook for Jonas Vingegaard. His old area was circled by moving slants, green fields, and winding roads ideal for a young cyclist. Denmark is known for its beautiful scenes and pleasing climate, and Jonas participated in every last bit of it.

Since the beginning, Jonas valued exploring the outside. His family would often go on bike rides together, making it a silliness and interesting time for them. They'd ride through the wonderful open nation, stopping at overwhelming towns and participating in the normal air. These rides were not just about getting from one spot then onto the following; they were connected to hanging out and having a few great times.

The Danish atmospheric conditions could be entirely alterable, with brilliant days and swirling ones. However, Jonas didn't let that stop him. He sorted out some way to ride his bike in an extensive variety of environments, which helped him with transforming into a more grounded and more gifted cyclist. Turbulent days inferred sprinkling through puddles, while brilliant days were unmistakably appropriate for longer rides.

In school, Jonas was known for being red hot and vigorous. He was continually anxious to share stories about his bike rides and examine his cycling legends. His associates and teachers could see how vivacious he was connected to cycling, and they maintained his dreams.

Encountering adolescence in Denmark gave Jonas the best environment to cultivate his love for cycling. The magnificent view, solid family, and dynamic lifestyle all had a significant effect in trimming him into the surprising cyclist he would transform into.

Experiencing youth in Denmark seemed to be living in a storybook for Jonas Vingegaard. His old region was included by moving slopes, green fields, and winding streets — ideal for a youthful cyclist. Denmark is known for its perfect scenes and satisfying environment, and Jonas partook in each and every piece of it.

Very quickly, Jonas regarded looking at the outside. His family would routinely go on bicycle rides together, making it a preposterous and unique time for them. They'd ride through the superb open country, finishing at surprising towns and partaking in the ordinary air. These rides were not just about getting started with one spot then onto the accompanying; they were associated with hanging out and having a couple of extraordinary times.

The Danish weather conditions could be no doubt alterable, with splendid days and twirling ones. In any case, Jonas didn't let that stop him. He figured out a good method for riding his bicycle in a broad assortment of climates, which assisted him with changing into a more grounded and more talented cyclist. Tempestuous days proposed sprinkling through puddles, while splendid days were clearly proper for longer rides.

In school, Jonas was known for being blasting and searing. He was consistently restless to share stories about his bicycle rides and inspect his cycling legends. His companions and instructors could perceive how exuberant he was associated with cycling, and they kept up with his fantasies.

Experiencing immaturity in Denmark gave Jonas the best climate to empower his affection for cycling. The extraordinary view, strong family, and dynamic way of life all had a huge impact in trimming him into the stunning cyclist he would change into.

Jonas Vingegaard tracked down his friendship for cycling to such an extent that numerous kids do — through fundamental, merry experiences. Everything started when he was outstandingly young, riding his most vital bike around his area. His little red bike wasn't just a toy; it was a section to a vast expanse of involvement.

As Jonas advanced around, he felt a sensation of chance and energy that was hard to beat. The breeze directly before him and the speed of the ride made him feel stimulated and euphoric. It wasn't a long time before he comprehended that journeying was some different option from a wonderful development — it was something he truly loved.

Right when Jonas was something like seven years old, he joined a cycling club. This was a significant stage for him. The club was overflowing with kids who were much the same way as amped in the mood for cycling as he was. Together, they chipped away at riding, gained new capacities, and battled in cheerful races. These activities made Jonas' veneration for cycling significantly more grounded.

He furthermore started watching cycling races on TV and looking into notable cyclists. He regarded their capacities and dreams of one day running nearby them. This persuaded him to work significantly more perseveringly and put his attention on transforming into an exceptional cyclist himself.

Cycling promptly transformed into a significant piece of Jonas' life. It was a side interest as well as an energy that filled him with elation and reason. Each bike ride, each race, and each new capacity gained made him fall more captivated by the game. This significant love for cycling was the support of all that Jonas would continue to achieve as a chief.

CHAPTER 2 THE START OF A CYCLING JOURNEY

The beginning of Jonas Vingegaard's cycling process was loaded up with fervor and assurance. At the point when he was around eight years of age, he started to view his energy for trekking more in a serious way. Which began as a great movement transformed into an excursion loaded up with new difficulties and open doors.

Jonas' folks saw his energy for cycling and chose to help him much more. They selected him in a neighborhood cycling club, where he met different children who shared his adoration for the game. The club was where Jonas could gain from experienced mentors, practice his abilities, and make new companions who were similarly as amped up for cycling as he was.

One of Jonas' first huge achievements was partaking in quite a while absolute first race. He was anxious yet in addition excited to contend. The race was a blend of euphoria and nerves, however it was a significant stage in his excursion. He didn't come out on top in that race, however he gained some useful knowledge and was much more spurred to move along.

Preparing turned into a major piece of Jonas' daily practice. He worked on riding consistently, dealing with his speed, equilibrium, and perseverance. He figured out how to deal with various sorts of territory and how to keep on track during long rides. His mentors showed him significant methods and methodologies that would help him in ongoing races.

Jonas' diligent effort paid off as he saw upgrades. He began coming out on top in neighborhood races and earning respect for his ability. Every triumph, large or little, made him more certain and amped up for what lay ahead.

The beginning of Jonas' cycling process was only the start of a surprising experience. Fully backed up by his family, the direction of his mentors, and his own assurance, he was well en route to turning into a surprising cyclist.

Jonas Vingegaard's most important bike ride was a preview of pure fulfillment and enthusiasm. Right when he was just a little youngster, his people gave him a little, brilliant red bike. It was anything but a thing luxurious, yet to Jonas, it was a fortune.

On that outright first ride, Jonas wobbled a piece as he became adjusted to changing on two wheels. The bike felt colossal and new, yet he was restless to research. With his people pulling for him, Jonas cut off down the walkway, his heart running with intensity.

As he sped up, his overall environmental factors seemed to open up. The impression of moving progressively quick was animating. The breeze whooshed past his face, and he felt an invigorating sensation of chance. Notwithstanding the way that he was riding just around the block, it appeared to be an amazing encounter.

Jonas' people were somewhat close with him, running nearby and offering elevating explanations. They observed gladly as he gained sureness, controlling around corners and sorting out some way to effortlessly dial back. Every last accomplishment made him smile, essentially more noteworthy.

That first bike ride was a supernatural experience. It was the beginning of a love for cycling that would grow further over the long haul. It wasn't just a ride, it was the start of a journey that would take Jonas to new spots and lead him to transform into a legendary cyclist.

Right when Jonas Vingegaard joined his close by cycling club, it meant an astounding new part in his journey. The club was an enthusiastic neighborhood energetic cyclist who shared his energy for traveling, and it was here that Jonas' friendship for the game began to sprout more impressively.

The important day at the club was both invigorating and fairly unnerving. Jonas met his new associates, who were all restless to ride and work on their capacities. The tutors welcomed him generously and got a handle on how the club worked. They examined informative gatherings, races, and how much fun it was to be significant for a gathering.

Planning with the club was one more experience for Jonas. He sorted out some way to ride even more, handle different sorts of scenes, and work on his speed. The tutors showed him huge strategies, from how to make sharp moves to how to stay steady on extensive rides. Each preparing meeting was a mix of learning and playing, and Jonas expected every single one.

The club moreover had normal races and events where Jonas could test his capacities and opponent others. These races were fortifying and a piece testing, yet they helped Jonas with seeing the sum he was getting to a higher level. Beating the competition in a race or achieving a singular best filled him with fulfillment and motivation.

Being significant for the club suggested some different options from planning and running. Jonas made new colleagues who shared his energy for cycling. They would visit about their #1 bikes, share tips, and engage each other during races. The connection and sponsorship from his partners made each ride essentially more pleasant.

Joining the local cycling club was a tremendous step for Jonas. It outfitted him with the capacities, data, and support he expected to create as a cyclist. The experiences and family relationships he gained there were urgent in framing him into the talented and concluded cyclist he would transform into.

CHAPTER 3 TRAINING HARD

As Jonas Vingegaard developed more focused on cycling, he realized that turning into a top cyclist required something other than riding for no particular reason. Preparing hard turned into a fundamental piece of his daily practice, and he moved toward it with devotion and excitement.

Every day, Jonas followed an organized preparation plan intended to make him a superior cyclist. His routine included various sorts of activities to develop fortitude, speed, and perseverance. He invested energy in his bicycle rehearsing different strategies, like climbing slopes, running, and making sharp turns.

These abilities were pivotal for taking care of various race conditions.

One critical part of his preparation was figuring out how to proficiently ride. Jonas dealt with his accelerating procedure to ensure he was involving his energy in the most effective way conceivable. He works on keeping a consistent speed, which is significant for long rides and races. This assisted him with remaining solid all through the whole race and not tire out excessively fast.

Off the bicycle, Jonas zeroed in on practices that developed his muscles. He did exercises like running, swimming, and strength preparing to keep his body in top shape. Solid legs, a sound heart, and great in general wellness assisted him with riding quicker and longer.

Jonas likewise scholarly the significance of legitimate sustenance and rest. Eating good food sources gave him the energy he expected to prepare hard, and getting sufficient rest permitted his body to recuperate and develop further. His mentors focused on that dealing with his body was similarly essentially as significant as rehearsing on the bicycle.

Preparing hard wasn't simple all of the time. There were days when Jonas felt drained or confronted difficulties, however his assurance made all the difference for him. He realized that all of exertion would assist him with improving as a cyclist. The difficult work paid off as he kept on improving, acquiring certainty and abilities that would lead him to future triumphs.

Through committed preparing, Jonas changed from a youthful cyclist enthusiastically for trekking into a gifted and serious rider. His obligation to try sincerely and continually improve was critical to his turn of events and accomplishments in the realm of cycling.

For Jonas Vingegaard, gaining from his mentors was a critical piece of his excursion to turning into a cycling champion. His mentors were something other than educators; they were coaches who assisted him with figuring out the complexities of going and directed him through each phase of his turn of events.

At the point when Jonas initially joined the cycling club, he was acquainted with experienced mentors who had an abundance of information about the game. These mentors saw potential in Jonas and were anxious to assist him with developing. They started by showing him the rudiments of cycling methods, for example, how to deal with the bicycle, how to change gears without a hitch, and how to keep a consistent speed.

As Jonas' abilities improved, his mentors gave further development. They showed him how to ride effectively in various circumstances, whether it was climbing steep slopes or hustling in the breeze. They told him the best way to settle on essential choices during races, similar to when to push hard and when to ration energy. This strategic information was vital for contending at a more significant level.

Perhaps the most significant example Jonas gained from his mentors was the significance of defining objectives. They assisted him with putting forth both transient objectives, such as further developing his lap times, and long haul objectives, like coming out on top in races. Having clear objectives kept Jonas roused and zeroed in on what he needed to accomplish.

Mentors likewise assumed a major part in assisting Jonas with remaining positive and certain. They gave consolation and valuable input, praising his triumphs and assisting him with gaining from his errors. Whenever Jonas confronted difficulties or misfortunes, his mentors were there to offer help and direction, assisting him with keeping focused.

Past the specialized parts of cycling, Jonas' mentors showed him the significance of sportsmanship and cooperation. They underlined that being a decent contender implied regarding others, cooperating with partners, and continuously endeavoring to put forth a valiant effort.

Gaining from his mentors was an indispensable piece of Jonas Vingegaard's development as a cyclist. Their aptitude, consolation, and backing assisted him with refining his abilities, remaining propelled, and accomplishing his fantasies in the realm of cycling.

For Jonas Vingegaard, practice was the best approach to transforming into a productive cyclist. Especially like sorting out some way to play an instrument or glorifying a game, practice was crucial for dealing with his capacities and achieving his goals.

Close to the beginning, practice suggested focusing on his bike reliably. Jonas would ride for a critical distance, managing his speed, balance, and control. Each preparing meeting helped him with getting better at dealing with his bike and riding capably. Whether he was practicing sharp turns, slant climbs, or running, all of the preparation made a difference.

Consistency was critical. Jonas understood that practicing regularly helped him with creating courage and perseverance. Particularly like another ability, cycling anticipated that repetitive work would overwhelm. By riding regularly, he made muscle memory, which allowed him to perform better during races. The more he practiced, the more pleasant and gifted he became.

Practice similarly suggested acquiring from blunders and making upgrades. During preparing gatherings, Jonas would occasionally fight or not continue as well as he trusted. Instead of getting dissuaded, he included these minutes as picking up astounding entryways. His tutors and accomplices would help him with understanding what turned out seriously and how to fix it, making each preparing meeting a potential chance to create.

Despite genuine practice, Jonas moreover worked on mental preparation. Practice wasn't just about riding; it was connected to building sureness and staying on target. He chipped away at envisioning races and completely took into account methodology, which helped him with outstanding intellectually gathered and ready during certified contentions.

The meaning of preparing loosened up past the bike. Jonas sought after helpful schedules like pursuing great eating routines, staying hydrated, and getting adequate rest. These penchants were dire for staying aware of his energy and execution.

As a general rule, practice was the groundwork of Jonas Vingegaard's thriving. It was through given and dependable practice that he worked on his capacities, vanquished challenges, and achieved his dreams as a cyclist. His commitment to practicing reliably and acquiring from each gathering was a significant piece of what made him a chief.

CHAPTER 4 BIG RACES AND ACHIEVEMENTS

As Jonas Vingegaard's abilities to cycle continued to improve, he began participating in more prominent and more eminent races. These races were the minutes where all his steady exertion and commitment paid off, and they made immense accomplishments in his journey to transforming into a cycling champion.

One of Jonas' underlying critical races was an invigorating experience. Fighting with other gifted cyclists, he felt a mix of energy and worry. Each race was a preliminary of his capacities and confirmation.

He tried to remain focused, manage his energy, and seek after sagacious decisions. Finishing perfect in these races furnished him with an example of what it was like to fight at a more huge level and prodded him to keep on pushing himself.

As Jonas obtained knowledge, he started to dominate the competition in races and acquire affirmation. Winning wasn't just about crossing the ultimate objective first; it was in a manner about showing his improvement as a cyclist. Each win was an outcome of countless significant lengths of work on, planning, and assurance. His victories brought him prizes and grants as well as respect and significant regard from the cycling neighborhood.

Maybe the most exciting achievement in Jonas' livelihood was winning a huge cycling event, similar to the Visit de France. This grandiose race is known for its troublesome courses and strong competitors. Winning it was a gift from paradise for Jonas, and it showed his magnificent capacity and troublesome work. The victory was a happy second for Jonas as well concerning his family, partners, and fans who had maintained him on the way.

Tremendous races and achievements weren't just about the honors; they were in like manner open entryways for Jonas to spur others. His thriving showed young cyclists that with troublesome work and responsibility, they could achieve their own dreams. Each race and achievement was a wandering stone in his trip, making him a genuine model for attempting contenders.

Through gigantic races and basic achievements, Jonas Vingegaard showed that he was some different option from a capable cyclist — he was a settled big enchilada whose troublesome work and energy for the game made him stick out.

Jonas Vingegaard's most vital huge race was a fundamental second in his cycling job, signifying the change from neighboring competitions to a more raised degree of contention. This race was something past an event; it was a tremendous test that attempted all that he had learned and practiced.

The race was held in a huge, clamoring setting with various spectators and individual competitors. Jonas felt a blend of intensity and nerves as he sorted out for the event. It was his chance to see how well he could perform against other talented cyclists and to experience the quality of a critical challenge.

Before the race began, Jonas went through his standard pre-race plan. He truly saw his bike to ensure everything was in magnificent condition, broadened his muscles, and evaluated his framework with his coach. His coach reminded him to stay focused and go with quick decisions generally through the race.

Exactly when the race started, Jonas wrapped up, incorporated by various cyclists, all restless to succeed. The course was attempting, with turns, turns, and steep inclines that attempted his steadiness and capacities. Jonas expected to remain alert and speed himself mindfully to protect energy for the later bits of the race.

As the race progressed, Jonas did all that can be expected with it. He pushed through the shortcoming, used his planning to manage the serious scene, and sought after quick decisions during significant moments. Disregarding the way that he didn't dominate the competition in the race, the experience was extraordinarily significant. He finished in a respectable position and gained an overflow of contribution from battling at this more elevated level.

Participating in his most important critical race was an immense achievement for Jonas. It indicated the beginning of his outing into more serious cycling and gave him pieces of information and delineations that would be huge for future races. The race showed him the force of huge challenges and helped him with understanding what it took to battle at the significant level.

This first huge race was a basic accomplishment in Jonas Vingegaard's calling. It was an opportunity for him to display his capacities, gain understanding, and set up for future victories. The models he acquired and the confirmation he obtained from this race were pressing in trimming his manner to transform into a cycling champion.

Winning awards and enrichments was a thrilling and remunerating piece of Jonas Vingegaard's outing as a cyclist. Each award addressed the troublesome work, responsibility, and capacity he had put into his game, and they stepped up huge accomplishments in his employment.

Whenever Jonas initially won an award, it was a preview of pure rapture and pride. He had arranged hard, battled in testing races, and put in unending extended lengths of preparing. Right when the results were accounted for, and his name was called as a champion, he felt a mix of enthusiasm and suspicion. Getting a handle on that prize was an unquestionable sign of his achievements and the progress he had made.

As Jonas continued to fight in extra races, he began to accumulate an arrangement of embellishments. Each improvement tended to a victory or a top finishing in an immense event. Whether it was a gold, silver, or bronze improvement, each one had its own uncommon spot in his heart. These designs weren't just polished praises; they were pictures of his responsibility and the challenges he had made due.

Winning awards and designs moreover brought Jonas affirmation inside the cycling neighborhood. His victories acquired him appreciation from various cyclists, guides, and fans. It was a way to deal with showing that his diligent exertion and getting ready were paying off, and it prodded him to keep on making a pass at significance.

For Jonas, each award was a celebration of his outing and achievements. They were a badge of the targets he had set and the work he had put into reaching them. Each award and embellishment was an exhibit of his mastery, assurance, and love for the game.

By and large, winning awards and embellishments was an undeniably exhilarating and critical piece of Jonas Vingegaard's cycling calling. They meant the triumphs and accomplishments along his way and filled in as a wellspring of inspiration and pride as he continued to pursue his dreams in cycling.

CHAPTER 5 LIFE AS A CHAMPION

Life as a supervisor for Jonas Vingegaard is a blend of troublesome work, strengthening experiences, and energizing minutes. Being a cycling champion goes with many awards and commitments that shape his ordinary daily schedule.

As a chief, Jonas participates in the affirmation and respect that go with his achievements. People value his commitment and capacities, and he regularly winds up at the focal point of consideration, whether it's giving gatherings, going to events, or meeting fans. This affirmation is an exhibit of his persistent exertion and accomplishment, yet it moreover suggests he wants to stay focused and keep on truly locking in.

Getting ready stays a gigantic piece of Jonas' life. For sure, even as a chief, he truly needs to stay in brilliant condition, so his ordinary timetable consolidates exhaustive educational courses. These gatherings help him with staying aware of his capacities, collect determination, and plan for approaching races. He works personally with his coaches to refine his techniques and stay before his adversaries.

Life as a supervisor moreover incorporates going out to various races and events all around the planet. Jonas will visit better places, experience new social orders, and meet individual cyclists. While journeying can be empowering, it also requires mindful planning and changing time among races and rest.

Regardless of the notoriety and involved plan, Jonas endeavors to keep a solid way of life. He contributes energy with friends and family, appreciates side interests, and requires minutes to loosen up and recharge. Staying aware of these affiliations helps him with remaining grounded and assists him with recalling the genuinely strong organization that helped him with achieving his dreams.

Being a manager moreover infers being a genuine model for young cyclists and fans. Jonas propels others with his story and shows that with troublesome work and affirmation, they likewise can achieve their goals. He often participates in neighborhood, school visits, and great objective rides, sharing his experiences and engaging others to follow their dreams.

Life as a manager is a rewarding adventure stacked up with troubles and wins. For Jonas Vingegaard, it's connected to participating in the accomplishment he's secured, continuing to improve, and stirring others while staying steady with his energy for cycling.

Winning is an extraordinary tendency for Jonas Vingegaard, a second stacked up with a mix of sentiments that blend joy, help, and pride. Each win tends to the completion of months or even extended lengths of troublesome work, getting ready, and responsibility.

Right when Jonas crosses the ultimate objective first, the hidden sensation is a flood of happiness. The troublesome work he has set into getting ready and making arrangements for the race has paid off, and the pride is overwhelming. There's a significant part of the time a preview of distrust, as he takes in the reality of winning and the celebration that follows.

The impression of winning is moreover significantly fulfilling. It's an affirmation of his mastery, relentlessness, and commitment to the game. The cheers from the gathering, the tribute from accomplices and competitors, and the enthusiasm existing separated from all the other things all add to a sensation of win and endorsement. Each win is an update that his undertakings have not solely been viable yet in that frame of mind by others.

Winning in a like manner brings a freeing sensation. The strain and assumption preparing for the race can be outrageous, and achieving a win is a way to deal with overcoming those troubles. The troublesome work and relinquishes put forth on the way merit the attempt when the result is a triumph.

Another basic piece of winning is conferring pleasure to others. Jonas habitually celebrates with his gathering, coaches, and family, who have maintained him all through his journey. Their ecstasy and pride in his success add to the enthusiasm and make the victory fundamentally more uncommon.

For Jonas, winning isn't just about the awards and embellishments; it's about the journey and the minutes preparing for it. It's connected to showing to himself that he can achieve his goals and making his dreams a reality. Winning is an area of strength that empowers his energy for cycling and moves him to continue to have a go at significance.

Jonas Vingegaard's flourishing as a cycling champion loosens up past his own achievements; it in like manner allows him the important opportunity to have a helpful result on others. Using his thriving to help and stir others is a huge piece of his journey.

One way Jonas helps others is by filling in as a genuine model. His record of troublesome work, dedication, and consistency rouses young cyclists and longing contenders. By sharing his experiences and showing what's possible truly and effort, he asks others to seek after their dreams and work towards their targets.

Jonas is also connected with various neighborhood philanthropic activities. He partakes in events that expose issues and resources for critical causes, for instance, prosperity drives, youth undertakings, and cycling-related establishments. His commitment brings up these causes and supports affiliations that have an impact in people's lives.

Despite his public appearances, Jonas much of the time attracts fans and energetic cyclists through schools and sports programs. He could visit schools to discuss his outing and the potential gains of troublesome work and assurance. These affiliations give huge models and convince youngsters to stay dynamic, set forth targets, and really trust themselves.

Jonas' thriving moreover allows him to add to the improvement of the game. By supporting area cycling clubs and tasks, he gives open ways to energetic contenders to plan and battle. His commitment can provoke redesigns in resources and support for developing cyclists, permitting them a better open door than success.

As a general rule, assisting others with his thriving is a huge piece of Jonas Vingegaard's calling. His undertakings to energize, backing, and add to critical makes reflect his obligation having a helpful result, both inside the cycling neighborhood then some.

CHAPTER 6 JONAS TIPS FOR YOUNG CYCLISTS

Jonas Vingegaard's excursion to turning into a cycling champion is loaded up with important examples. Here are a few hints he imparts to youthful cyclists to help them on their own way to progress:

Put forth Clear Objectives: Jonas encourages youthful cyclists to define explicit and reachable objectives. Whether it's working on an individual best, learning another method, or coming out on top in a neighborhood race, having clear objectives helps keep you spurred and centered.

Practice Routinely: Steady practice is critical to progress. Jonas accentuates the significance of riding routinely to construct abilities, perseverance, and certainty. Indeed, even on days when you feel tired, rehearsing assists you with improving.

Relax: Having some good times while cycling is significant. Jonas urges youthful cyclists to partake during the time spent learning and riding. At the point when you love what you're doing, it causes all the difficult work to feel advantageous.

Gain from Missteps: No one's perfect, and it's a characteristic piece of learning. Jonas recommends seeing mix-ups as any open doors to learn and develop. Dissect what turned out badly, change, and continue to push ahead.

Remain Positive: An uplifting outlook can have a major effect. Jonas encourages youthful cyclists to remain perky, in any event, when confronted with difficulties or misfortunes. Having confidence in yourself and keeping an uplifting perspective assists you with beating impediments.

Pay attention to Your Mentors: Mentors give significant direction and input. Jonas urges youthful cyclists to listen cautiously to their mentors, heed their guidance, and clarify pressing issues assuming they're uncertain about something.

Deal with Your Body: Legitimate nourishment, hydration, and rest are fundamental for execution and recuperation. Jonas stresses the significance of practicing good eating habits, remaining hydrated, and getting sufficient rest to keep your body in top shape.

Have Tolerance: Turning into a talented cyclist takes time and exertion. Jonas reminds youthful competitors to show restraint toward their advancement and comprehend that improvement comes step by step.

Support Your Colleagues: Cycling isn't just about individual achievement; it's likewise about collaboration. Jonas urges youthful cyclists to help and empower their colleagues, as collaboration and kinship are significant pieces of the game.

Remain Inquisitive: Continue learning and investigating new methods and procedures. Jonas encourages youthful cyclists to remain inquisitive and receptive, continuously searching for ways of improving and extending their insight into the game.

These tips from Jonas Vingegaard can assist youthful cyclists with fostering their abilities, remain persuaded, and partake in their excursion in the realm of cycling.

Getting all that going in cycling is a surprising encounter! Here is a clear manual for help young cyclists with beginning their trip:

Find the Right Bike: Start with a bike that obliges your size and is sensible for your riding needs. For tenderfoots, a well-fitted bike is crucial for comfort and control. You can visit a local bike search for counsel on picking the right bike.

Secure Central Capacities: Begin by dominating fundamental abilities to travel, such as changing, coordinating, and dialing back. Work on riding in a secured, open locale like an entertainment region or a quiet street. Start with short rides and logically increase the distance as you become more certain.

Wear Security Stuff: Prosperity is critical! Ceaselessly wear a cap to defend your head. Depending upon where you ride, you could in like manner consider wearing gloves, knee pads, and elbow pads for added security.

Join a Close by Club: Quest for a local cycling club or assembling. Joining a club can give you induction to experienced guides, pack rides, and events. It's similarly an inconceivable technique for meeting other energetic cyclists and making new friends.

Set forth Little Targets: Start with pretty much nothing, possible goals to remain stirred. This could be something clear, for example, sorting out some way to ride without planning wheels or completing a particular distance. Acclaim your headway and set forth new goals as you move along.

Practice Regularly: Dependable practice helps you with building capacities and assurance. Endeavor to ride multiple times every week, whether or not it's just for a short distance. The more you practice, the better you'll transform into.

Learn Bike Backing: Fundamental bike upkeep is significant. Sort out some way to check your bike's tire pressure, oil the chain, and improve on fixes. Keeping your bike with everything looking good ensures a smoother and safer ride.

Take Representations: If possible, ponder taking models from a coach or instructor. They can show you authentic systems, bike managing capacities, and security tips. Delineations can assist you with chipping away at speedier and ride even more unquestionably.

Have A few great times: specifically, live it up! Participate in the open door and experience that cycling brings. Examine new courses, challenge yourself, and value the experience of riding.

Stay Safe: Reliably comply with some safe rules, for instance, riding with traffic, using hand banners, and observing your ecological components. Respect other road clients and be cautious while riding.

Starting in cycling is a remunerating experience that opens up a vast expanse of possible results. With the right bike, prosperity stuff, and practice, you can set out on a fascinating journey and track down the enjoyment of cycling.

Troublesome work is a groundwork of progress in any field, including cycling. For Jonas Vingegaard, troublesome work expected a fundamental part in achieving his dreams and transforming into a cycling champion. Here is the explanation troublesome work is so critical:

Capacity Headway: Troublesome work helps you with chipping away at your capacities. In cycling, this suggests effective financial planning energy practicing methodology, building diligence, and refining your capacities to ride. The more effort you put in, the better you become.

Overcoming Hardships: Cycling can be extraordinary, with irksome domains and testing races. Troublesome work helps you with pushing through these challenges, gathering strength, and overcoming obstacles that come your way.

Creating Mettle and Determination: Result in cycling requires genuine strength and perseverance. Common and committed getting ready develops your muscles, fabricates your steadiness, and sets you up for long rides and serious races.

Achieving Targets: Spreading out and showing up at goals requires liability and effort. Whether you're intending to additionally foster your race times, win a contention, or master another skill, troublesome work is central to achieving these targets.

Securing Assurance: When you attempt genuinely and see the delayed consequences of your undertakings, it upholds your conviction. Troublesome work prompts improvement and accomplishment, which develops your trust in your abilities and rouses you to forge ahead.

Learning and Improvement: Troublesome work incorporates reliable learning and changing. As you train and fight, you gain from your experiences, refine your strategies, and create as a cyclist. This persistent course of progress is driven by dedication and effort.

Building Discipline: Troublesome work shows discipline and fixation. It requires sticking to a planning plan, managing your time, as a matter of fact, and staying committed regardless, while trying. These attributes are huge both in cycling and in various ordinary issues.

Acquiring Appreciation: Troublesome work is regularly seen and respected by others. In the cycling neighborhood, responsibility and effort secure the regard of colleagues, coaches, and fans. It shows that you're influential for the game and zeroed in on your success.

Setting out Open entryways: Troublesome work opens approaches to new entryways. Whether it's battling in more prominent races, joining a cycling group, or gaining sponsorships, your work and responsibility create open doors for improvement and movement.

10. Participating in the Trip: Troublesome work makes the outing truly fulfilling. The satisfaction of showing up at your goals and gaining ground is overhauled by the work you've put in. It makes every accomplishment more huge and satisfying.

By and large, troublesome work is principal for gaining ground in cycling and another pursuit. It helps you with cultivating your capacities, rout troubles, and show up at your goals. For Jonas Vingegaard, troublesome work was an essential part of his outing to transform into a legend, and it's a huge delineation for anyone trying to achieve their dreams.

CONCLUSION

Jonas Vingegaard's journey from a young cycling enthusiast to a world-renowned champion is a powerful testament to the values of hard work, perseverance, and passion. His story serves as an inspiring example of how dedication and commitment can transform dreams into reality.

Starting with a love for cycling, Jonas's early days were filled with simple joys and a growing fascination with the sport. His journey was marked by significant milestones, from his first bike ride to joining a local cycling club. Each step was crucial in shaping his skills and nurturing his talent. His experiences taught him the importance of setting goals, practicing regularly, and learning from every challenge he faced.

The role of his coaches was instrumental in guiding him through the complexities of competitive cycling. Their expertise, encouragement, and support provided Jonas with the tools he needed to excel. Through their guidance, he learned not only the technical aspects of cycling but also the strategic and mental components required for success.

Training became a central part of Jonas's routine, with each session designed to push his limits and refine his abilities. He understood that becoming a better cyclist required consistent effort and a willingness to learn. His dedication to training and improvement showcased the importance of discipline and resilience in achieving excellence.

Participating in big races was both exhilarating and demanding. Each race was a test of Jonas's preparation and skill, offering opportunities to showcase his talent and compete against the best. Winning trophies and medals brought immense satisfaction, recognizing his hard work and affirming his position as a top cyclist. Yet, these achievements were not merely personal victories but also opportunities to inspire and give back.

Jonas's success extended beyond his own accomplishments. By helping others, he demonstrated the value of using one's platform for positive impact.

Whether through community involvement, supporting young athletes, or contributing to charitable causes, his success became a means to uplift and motivate others.

For young cyclists and aspiring athletes, Jonas's journey offers valuable lessons. Setting clear goals, practicing diligently, staying positive, and embracing the support of coaches are essential steps toward achieving one's dreams. His story underscores that hard work is not just about physical training but also about building character, overcoming obstacles, and continuously striving for improvement.

Jonas Vingegaard's rise to cycling stardom is a compelling narrative of passion, hard work, and perseverance. His achievements highlight the rewards of dedication and the importance of remaining committed to one's goals. As he continues to inspire others, his legacy serves as a reminder that with determination and effort, any dream can be realized. His journey is a celebration of the spirit of cycling and the boundless possibilities that come with pursuing one's passions with unwavering resolve.

Thank for reading

Printed in Dunstable, United Kingdom